Giant Slayers

Desmon R. Daniel, PhD.

Dedication

To those on whose shoulders I stand

FOREWORD

My late father often recited a simple saying to me when I was confronted with challenges as a youth. He would say, "It's time to meet the bully in the field!" Needless to say, voluntarily embarking upon such a potentially cataclysmic undertaking did not sound the least bit appealing to me. However, I grew to understand that life's challenges would not go away merely because I was unwilling to meet them. To the contrary, our unwillingness to meet troubling situations often results in them growing in dimension. Even when presented with challenges that are "giant," we must confront them as David did Goliath. In this book Dr. Daniel provides keen spiritual (and secular) insight into recognizing and confronting the giants who will no doubt confront us during our lifetime. More importantly, Dr. Daniel addresses the spiritual and mental preparation required of us to appropriately confront these daunting behemoths.

Although I have known Dr. Daniel since childhood, I was as surprised as I was humbled when he requested that I write the foreword to this important piece of literature. Through my long association with Dr. Daniel he has come to know me (and my many flaws) perhaps better than anyone. Indeed, I thought – couldn't he have found a more perfect individual to assist him in this significant endeavor? However, after having had the opportunity to read "Giant Slayer," I now understand that this book will benefit admittedly "flawed individuals" (such as myself), as well as those who have less flaws and face fewer challenges. Simply put, this book speaks to confronting problems that we are guaranteed to face.

Growing up in Saginaw, Michigan was extremely challenging. Saginaw is a small blue-collar town whose economic base was ravaged as a consequence of the decline of the automobile industry. This economic decline also consequentially wreaked havoc on the social fabric of the community. Each day brought real challenges. Sadly, many of our peers met Calamitous and irreversible fates as a consequence of making the proverbial "wrong" decision when confronting their respective giants. Despite having loving parents who wanted the best for (and from) us, neither Dr. Daniel nor myself were exempt from having to make critical and potentially life-altering decisions. Indeed, each day we confronted problems – some with larger dimensions than others. These problems are figuratively akin to the giant, "Goliath," confronted by David. No matter their form, these giants are real and how we confront them will make the difference in the quality of our physical and spiritual lives. Remember, although these giants are daunting, there is simply no avoiding them. Most assuredly, in life, "problems will come."

Although Dr. Daniel and I successfully navigated the challenges of our youth, we quickly came to understand that "giants" are omnipresent and not confined to the geographical boundaries of Saginaw. As an adult, Dr. Daniel has met one personal challenge and tragedy after the next. Despite these challenges Dr. Daniel has remained resolute in his commitment to overcome the current challenge while preparing himself spiritually to meet the **next** giant. Dr. Daniel has repeatedly and unflinchingly met countless bullies in the field. He has returned to Saginaw and has embarked upon the task of ensuring that young people in the community have an ally to prepare them for their inevitable encounters with these unrelenting giants. Because of this book, we also are now the beneficiaries of Dr. Daniel's battlefield experiences. If you desire to be better prepared to meet your bully, in your field, read on...

Jeffrey A. Taylor

Giant Slayers

As a young boy growing up in mid-west America I can vividly recall growing up in a home filled with love, joy, peace, and certainly our share of storms. Each of these areas brought forth rich experiences that have shaped my life. Today I am mature enough to admit that some of the most powerful and enriching experiences have come through adversity. A wise man once told me that life is filled with experiences that are intended to mold our character like the master potter molds a fine work of art on the wheel. The clay is expected to yield itself to the master potter as the clay is molded into its final shape and form. The clay is so obedient to the point that if a flaw arises the master potter has the freedom to break down the clay with one motion and start the process all over again. The clay has no will of its own, the clay exist to experience the joy of being made, and the subsequent use for its intended purpose.

In this life our total conscious is made of a collection of experiences that will teach and guide us to our next station in life. At a young age I was exposed to the benefits of a formal education. That is not to say that formal education is the rule by which we should measure our success, however, it is true that in America we spend an average of 30 hours a week in school with people whom we generally do not live. Thus it can be argued that our experience with the world is generally shaped through the lens of educational experiences. One of my earliest memories of school is one that was shaped through adversity.

I recall climbing a huge ladder to the top of a slide. Each rung of the ladder allowed me to get closer and closer to the blissful joy of sliding freely for what seemed like a lifetime. More often than not I would land safely on my frail behind, yet I would jump up and brush myself off before heading back to my rightful place in line. Yet one day I climbed to the top of the ladder, as I had so many times before, only to be pushed down to the ground. Upon hitting the ground I received the attention of the school staff and eventually went to the doctor where I was given the necessary treatment. To this day, I look at the photos of my youth and simply shake my head at the photos of me wearing a sky blue mouth protector. This is my first memory of coming into contact with a giant.

You see the giant wanted my place in line and decided to take it by force. Today I know that the kingdom of heaven suffereth violence and the violent take it by force. Please don't confuse this introduction as a promotion of physical violence; Lord knows we have enough of that in the world today. Instead open your spirit to receive this call to action. Instead of picking up your weapons of destruction I encourage you to pick up your sling and your stone and boldly take aim at the giants that continue to plague your home, your community, your school, your job, and your country.

Arguably, one of the highly prolific warriors most commonly known to us is David. You know David, the guy who was said to be a man after God's own heart. What exactly made David a man after God's own heart is a subject of great theological debate. My intention is not to enter into this great debate; I simply want to recall some experiences of biblical proportions in light of the many challenges facing believers, like David, even now.

CHAPTER ONE

Our God Is an AWESOME God

It has been said that our God is an AWESOME God. The truth is that there is no end to the magnitude of God. There is nothing finite about neither God nor God's love for those who believe. Throughout time God has demonstrated an infinite love for humanity. In fact it can be argued that God has changed both natural and physical laws in order to bring some of man's greatest challenges into focus. However, some things that have happened were never intended.

The Bible acknowledges two groups of giants, Nephilim and Rephaim, both of which were displeasing unto God. This race of giants appears in the Old Testament or Hebrew Bible (I will use the term Old Testament). They were born as a result of the union of "the sons of God" and "the daughters of men." The Nephilim are said to be the descendants of famous rulers and valiant warriors existing prior to the flood. Rephaim dwelled in Palestine prior to the time of Abraham. They were known by names like Emims (Deuteronomy 2:11) and Zamzummims (Deuteronomy 2:20) Like the Nephilim they were characterized as valiant warriors partly due to their tremendous physical stature.

The union of giants and humans disrupted God's order and from that time until the present we have been forced to deal with giants in our midst.

> Giants: Human beings of abnormal size and strength. Races of giants are first mentioned in the Old Testament in Genesis 6:4 where giant god like beings was produced by the union of "the son's of God" and the "daughters of men." These giants or Nephilim, became "mighty men...men of renown," probably a reference to their tremendous height. These abnormal unions displeased God (Genesis 6:5-6)." –Nelsons Bible Dictionary

Today our giants do not appear with the same physical features as recorded in the Bible, therefore, their presence requires further examination. History has recorded some of the most dynamic and spectacular events known to mankind, none more prolific than the

Biblical accounts of the Hebrews and early believers. One of the earliest recordings of bravery, cunning and faith can be found in the first book of Samuel. This book records the bravery of young David, the boy who fought the lion, David the boy who fought the bear. David, the boy who was destined to fight for his family, his country, and his faith.

History records that David slew Goliath, a mighty Philistine known throughout the land. Goliath of Gath is commonly known as a biblical warrior famous for his battle against a much smaller David. A brief review of the literature reveals some notable and distinct differences between primary contextual resources specifically the Masoretic (Hebrew), Septuagint (Greek), and Dead Sea Scrolls accounts. For our purposes we will rely primarily on the Hebrew Bible as the biblical account.

According to the biblical account; during the reign of Saul twice a day for forty days Goliath, the Philistines mighty champion, would approach the Israelite flanks and issue a challenge. Goliaths physical stature is debatable; some say he stood "four cubits and a span" which translates to some 198 centimeters or about 6 foot 6 inches. The Masoretic texts give the height of "six cubits and a span" that would make Goliath 290 centimeters equivalent to 9 foot 6 inches tall. It would be sufficient to say that this guy was huge.

So twice a day this huge guy would come out to talk trash to the Israelites. This went on for forty days like clock work. Goliath would come out in the morning and evening saying "send out a champion of your own so that we may battle to the death to determine the victor." Until this point Saul and the Israelites were afraid to respond.

One day David shows up with lunches for his brothers. He hears that Saul has promised a reward to any man that will defeat Goliath the Philistine champion. David also witnesses Goliath talking trash first hand and decides to take them both up on their respective offers. After some time David is able to convince Saul to allow him to represent the Israelites. Saul insists that David wear his armor, however, David is more insistent that he retain the services of his trusty sling and five smooth stones which he would later retrieve from a nearby brook.

Can you believe this? I mean this is the stuff that movies are made of. Can't you just see it at the IMAX?

Wait, why would David need five smooth stones to bring down one giant? Sure he is characterized as mighty, valiant and great. After all God plus David is a majority. Surely David was a young boy of faith; his faith had historically brought him through many other challenging experiences. Remember this same kid fought a lion and a bear and won. It takes either a fool or someone filled with faith to wage a battle against either one of these formidable foes. I choose to believe that David represented the latter of the two, David was filled with faith.

So, if it is true that history has recorded some of the most dynamic and spectacular events known to man then surely this has to be one of them. Why would David select "five smooth stones" from the brook instead of just one? Certainly one well placed stone could take down this Goliath. Sure David was small in stature, but he was valiant of heart. You could say he had the heart of a lion and the tenacity of a bear. This Philistine Goliath was considered to be the fiercest of his nation. He represented countless people who coward at his physical prowess. According to the Complete Idiots Guide to The Bible Goliath stood more that 9 feet tall.

He wore over 125 pounds of armor. This guy was really huge. The tip of his spear was said to have weighed 15 pounds alone. You might think that a stone thrown at this guy might produce the first recorded home run with the tip of his spear.

Surely Jesse had to be concerned for his youngest boy who dared to face this giant with five smooth stones. This story is about more than conquering a giant. It's more than good verses evil, more than the triumph of the under dog or even the expression of intestinal fortitude. It's about trusting God everyday of our lives, it's about believing that God has ordained greatness and that God will do anything to ensure victory in the life of the believer.

CHAPTER TWO

Smooth vs. Slick

Decision/Dilemma

Will you choose your tongue and respond to the verbal threats of the giant with verbal gymnastics. Will you stand in the field and shout expletives, quote scriptures or perhaps cover your ears.

When faced with your giant what weapon will you choose.

In most cases we will resort to some familiar tactic, something that we feel comfortable with, something that we have used before with some level of success. Most often we choose to enter the battle focused on what we see. We focus so intently on what is before that we may even loose sight of the issues accompanying the Big problem. Goliath stood as the representative of a problem between two nations the Israelites and the Philistines. Goliath was merely a visual representation of a bigger problem. He represented a nation who laid siege on the most sacred object that the Israelites had. Goliath was a huge reminder that the Philistines had previously taken the "Ark of the Covenant" which contained the stone tablets Moses himself had put there.

Imagine someone breaking into your home and taking a precious heirloom that had been passed down from generation to generation. This heirloom was entrusted to you with the expectation that you would pass down its rich history and share the potential of its greatness for generations to come. Although they would regain possession of this great artifact, they certainly had reason to dislike the Philistines. I imagine it was difficult for the Israelites to see Goliath day after day calling them out only to see this ruddy little guy David go out to confront him with a sling and some "smooth stones."

The smooth stones represent composure. David's composure when confronting the giant was disarming. His composure created a level of cognitive dissonance that caused the giant to shake his head and become enraged. David's composure ticked off. The Goliath was insulted by the fact that the Israelites would send a boy to do a man's job. To add insult to injury this boy had no armor, no spear, no sword and no shield.

Again I ask you, what weapon will you choose when you are faced with your giant?

David chose five smooth stones and now we see the strength of the smooth stone. The smooth stone also represents preparation. We have no way of knowing how long this stone was in the stream. We don't know if it was transplanted as a result of an intentional movement or somehow washed down stream as a result of a storm or flood. What we do know is that it has been characterized as smooth. Smooth means there were no jagged edges or rough ends. We know that these smooth stones met another force which was arguably stronger than the stone itself and that force prepared the stone for its destiny.

The stone was a tool of faith. Faith shaped the stone by virtue of experience. Faith's experience transcends our understanding and works to shape the tools of our lives so that our tools can perform their intended works at a time that God has ordained.

David's selection of the five smooth stones exemplifies manifest destiny. Manifest destiny is experienced when we bring all of our gifts, talents, mind, will and emotions into our current situation. When we expose our innermost being to the challenge confronting our existence, confronting our existence beyond this very moment in time then and only then can we arm ourselves with our smooth stones.

> **Decision**
> What weapon will you choose?
> Will you rely on what is deep inside?

CHAPTER 3

Ishbi – benob vs. Abishai

II Samuel 21:15 - 17
(The Giant of Discouragement vs.
The Courage of God)

II Samuel 21:15 – 17 (KJV) Moreover the Philistines had yet war again with the Israel; and David went down, and his servants with him, and fought against the Philistines: and David waxed faint. 16 And Ishbi-benob, which was of the sons of the giant, the weight of whose spear weighed three hundred shekels of brass in weight, he being girded with a new sword, thought to have slain David. 17 But Abishai the son of Zeruiah succoured him and smote the Philistine, and killed him. Then the men

of David sware unto him, saying, Thou shalt go no more out with us to battle, that thou quench not the light of Israel.

(NIV) Once again there was a battle between the Philistines and Israel. David went down with his men to fight against the Philistines, and he became exhausted. 16 And Ishbi-Benob, one of the descendents of Rapha, whose bronze spearhead weighed three hundred shekels and who was armed with a new sword, said he would kill David. 17 But Abishai son of Zeruiah came to David's rescue: he struck the Philistine down and killed him. Then David's men swore to him saying. "Never again will you go out with us to battle, so that the lamp of Israel will not be extinguished."

(NLT) Once again the Philistines were at war with Israel. And when David and his men were in the thick battle, David became weak and exhausted. 16 Ishbi-benob was a descendant of the giants; his bronze spearhead weighed more than seven pounds, and he was armed with a new sword. He had cornered David and was about to kill him. 17 But Abishai son of Zeruiah came to his rescue and killed the Philistine. After that David's men declared, "You are not going out to battle again! Why should we risk snuffing out the light of Israel?"

(NASB) Now when the Philistines were at war again with Israel, David went down and his servants with him; and as they fought against the Philistines, David became weary. 16Then Ishbi-benob, who was among the descendants of the giant, the weight of whose spear was three hundred shekels of bronze in weight, was girded with a new sword, and he intended to kill David. 17But Abishai the son of Zeruiah helped him, and struck the Philistine and killed him. The men of David swore to him, saying, "You shall not go out again with us to battle, so that you do not extinguish the lamp of Israel."

Ishbi-benob, represent discouragement he said that he would kill David (the lamp of Israel). His plan was thwarted by Abishai (David's nephew).

**Abishai, is characterized as being fiercely coura-
geous and loyal to his uncle David, additionally he
was a fierce soldier who fought valiantly on behalf
of his people.**

The simple truth of the matter is that David was
prepared to confront the other "Giants." Other Giants…
what do you mean other Giants? II Samuel 21:15 – 22
records the existence of other Giants, the descendents of
Goliath. These descendents swore to avenge the death
of Goliath by killing David. Thus; the trash talking and
taunting and ridicule did not end with Goliath's demise,
it continued for generations to come.

It is interesting that our issues seem to have rela-
tive. Just when you think you have conquered one
issue here comes another. David realized that very fact
when he selected the five smooth stones. He realized,
through faith that all it took was one well placed stone
to bring down the mighty Goliath, but there would be
more battles to fight. Many believers are forced to deal
with the issues of their forefathers or other ancestors.
Remember that God spoke to the children of Israel and
told them "I the Lord thy God am a jealous God" visit-

ing the iniquity of the fathers upon the children unto the third and fourth generation of them that hate me; and showing mercy unto thousands of them that love me and keep my commandments." So in some sense it is logical that we would have issues to face which somehow mirror the issues of those who have come before us, especially when our loyalties are misplaced.

In a perfect world our ancestors, like David, left symbolic stones or tools that we could utilize to destroy the giants in our lives. However, due to the vicissitudes of life many of us are unfamiliar with our ancestral issues thus we become bound by them never having the opportunity to confront them and deal with the knowledge of our issues origin. Sometimes family allegiance can be problematic if we fail to analyze our situation, or confront the issues which are brought to our attention.

Imagine the advancement possible if we knew the origin of the first case of cancer, aids, autism, heck what about the common cold. Who ever coined the phrase "knowledge is power" was really on to something. In this case (discouragement vs. loyalty) we can trace the anger of the Philistines back to the death of their valiant hero Goliath who died at the hand of David.

As fate would have it another war arose between the Philistines and the Israelites. By this time David was King and he went down to fight against his arch enemies. Because of the fierce nature of the fight David became exhausted. During this exhaustive state the Philistines sought to avenge the death of their hero Goliath. They sent Ishbi-benob into battle on their behalf.

Ishbi-benob vowed to kill David. Ishbi-benob represents discouragement he sought to attack David at his weakest moment. Isn't it amazing how the simple things beset us when we are mentally, physically or emotionally drained? It is often at the time of our weakest moment that we are overthrown. In the physical realm our immune system is at its weakest after we are physically drained. After we have pulled an all nighter or worked a couple of double shifts or perhaps spent the last few days dealing with issues on the job or at home.

Imagine David's state, by this time he is older in age and more knowledgeable since his encounter with Goliath, knowledge comes at a cost. It can be said that wisdom is the application of knowledge. Hence the feminine reference to wisdom is found in the Book of Proverbs. In Proverbs we find that wisdom cry's out for the attention of humankind that we might hear her cry. In so doing we shall find that knowledge is greater than the choicest gold and that wisdom is worth more than precious rubies. Wisdom is therefore the application of knowledge.

That being said knowledge becomes even more critical. David knew there would be more giants, thus he wisely selected five smooth stones. With every battle comes knowledge, but why is it that many of us face the same or similar battles over and over again?

Enter Abishai, nephew of David, son of Zeruiah and brother of Joab. Abishai represents the Courage of God and loyalty in the face of discouragement. This giant (Ishbi-benob) discouragement carries tools or weapons that at first glance seem overwhelmingly powerful. Imagine approaching a foe whose bronze spearhead is said to weigh 300 shekels (the most common weight in Hebrew times which represents 100th of the weight that one man could carry). This foe engages in a series of behaviors or actions designed to discourage his opponent. Behaviors are not limited to yelling, cursing, pounding on his chest. Behaviors that may include wearing a belt fashioned with the thumbs of all his previous conquest. Thus the stench of his presence alone is unbearable causing people to flee.

Yet Abishai armed with the Courage of God entered his battlefield on behalf of the King destined to win. You see courage is the root of discourage. Courage must exist or the prefix (dis) has no meaning. It is the lack of courage that gives "dis" life. Abishai knew this and simply applied the principle of wisdom. Abishai knew based on past experience wherein he learned how and when to apply what he knew. He knew that it was natural for the enemy to attempt to disarm him with false behaviors intended to cause him to lose focus or a grand outburst designed to create a false sense of fear. He also knew courage was the head and that he possessed the power of God in battle.

The Bible teaches us that we are the head and not the tail and that we are above and not beneath. More importantly we find that all things are possible with God on our side. One application of this principle encourages us to rely on the wisdom of God and not on what we see with our eyes. One of the first examples of Gods response to our failure to rely on His plan for our lives is made evident in our ability to become discouraged.

This is exemplified in the 32nd chapter of Numbers. Here Moses admonishes the children of Gad and Reuben because they have become discouraged as did there ancestors when they were directed by God to go and see the land of God's (Jehovah's) promise. As a result of their discouragement God became angry and swore that none of the men from age twenty and up would see the land God previously promised unto Abraham, Isaac and Jacob. God expects the believer to wholly follow in spite of the obstacles of discouragement, in spite of what is appears, in spite of the ill report.

In the face of discouragement God expects that we would wholly rely on our relationship with God through Christ Jesus. This relationship hinges on the belief that God loves us so much that he gave his only begotten son to die on a cross that we might have a right to the tree of life. Old Testament scripture provides the believer with miracles wrought by the hand of God on behalf of the believer. These miracles should serve as the basis of our faith experience confirmed through the resurrection of Christ.

Today we are faced with the giant of discouragement as we look out on the condition of the world, however we (believers) are expected to holdfast to the promises of God. We have been promised that God through Jesus Christ would never leave us nor forsake us, in spite of the presence of the giant. In spite of the doctors report that our health is failing, in spite of the fact that someone does not believe in the promise that God has uttered to us in the midst of our adversity. God expects that we (individually and collectively) would respond to the wilds of the enemy with a Holy Ghost boldness that will cause the enemy to rise up and flee from our very presence.

One of the keys to defeating the giant of discouragement is exemplified in the life of Jesus Christ. When confronted by Satan who took him up to a high place after having fasted, Jesus was tempted in an attempt to discourage him from carrying out the will of God. Yet, Jesus knowing who he is in God rebuked Satan causing him to flee from his very presence.

Please know that God expects that we (individually and collectively) would fully exercise the measure of faith that has been given to us by Him. Know that your individual measure of faith is being nurtured and nourished through our relationship with God. The more we trust God, the more we rely on God, the more we acknowledge God the greater our resolve to act on the measure of faith given.

The strength of Abishai's character came to its full fruition when he was faced with the giant of discouragement. Abishai realized that no weapon formed by the hand of man could ever withstand the power of God. No matter how loud the giant exclaimed, no matter how big the weapon, no matter what previous reports may have been Abishai knew that he had to stand in the courage of God and exercise the measure of faith given him.

Today I ask you "what will you do when you are faced with the giant of discouragement?' Will you exercise the measure of faith given to you by the King of Kings and the Lord of Lord's or will you allow the trick of the enemy to give life to discouragement?

CHAPTER 4

Saph vs. Sibbecai

II Samuel 21:18
(The Giant of Destruction vs.
The Intervention of God)

II Samuel 21:18 (KJV) And it came to pass after this; that there was again a battle with the Philistines at Gob: then Sibbechai the Hushathite slew Saph, which was of the sons of the giant.

(NIV) In the course of time, there was another battle with the Philistines, at Gob. At that time Sibbecai the Hushathite killed Saph, on of the descendants of Rapha.

(NLV) After this, there was another battle against the Philistines at Gob. As they fought, Sibbecai from Hushah killed Saph, another descendant of the giants.

(NASB) Now it came about after this that there was war again with the Philistines at Gob; then Sibbecai the Hushathite struck down Saph, who was among the descendants of the giant.

It has been said that we exists within the confines of human condition which finds us in one of three states. We are either going into a situation, coming out of a situation or in the midst of a situation. The true test of ones character is found in the midst of this triangular experience.

It appears that the descendants of David were always at war with someone, just as we are in a perpetual state of movement. Each movement creates an opportunity to do better, be better, and to live better than ever before. Yet in the midst of our movement we are introduced to destructive forces whose sole purpose is to drive a wedge into our positive progress.

Sibbecai (sib'-be-kahee) is characterized as a mighty man. He represents the intervention of God which comes to us like a roaring lion. Sibbecai was considered a strong leader, he was given charge over 24,000 troops during the time of war. Anyone given authority over that many individuals has to have a strong sense of what is right and a stronger conviction to do what is right in spite of what is popular. This type of strength does not originate in man but it comes from God who it the author and finisher of our faith.

Sibbecai trusted not in his strength, knowledge or prowess he merely yielded himself to the God of Israel in carrying out his duties. He relied on the intervention of God. The Bible teaches us to acknowledge God in ALL our ways and trust that God will direct our path. One of the key words is ALL. All means to the inclusion of everything and the exclusion of nothing. Thus when we are confronted with our personal "Saph," our personal discouragement we are encouraged to acknowledge the God of Abraham, Isaac, and Jacob the God of all creation who is able to do exceedingly abundantly more than we could ever ask or think.

When we learn to rely on the intervention of God in

our lives, no matter where we find ourselves we give the Holy Spirit the opportunity to manifest a miracle or give rise to a testimony of the awesome power of God. One of the common characteristics found in the giants in our lives is their perceived power. You see the giant has limited real power, their power is seemingly absorbed from those whom they come in contact with. Because of the power we have given the giant by virtue of their make up (their size) the giant becomes larger and larger thus taking on the appearance of being insurmountable. We are then subjected to destruction because we have not yielded to the intervention of God, but instead we have yielded to the presence of the giant.

How many times have you been destroyed by your own doing? Perhaps it was a dream unfulfilled or an opportunity you talked yourself out of because you were afraid of the giant. I was told that Fear is simply **F**alse **E**vidence with an **A**ppearance of **R**eality. Many of our dreams and aspirations are aborted well before they have been given an opportunity to see the light of day.

It is incumbent upon every believer to know that you have the power to subdue the giant Saph, the giant of destruction. This giant seeks to kill, steal and destroy the God given dreams and aspirations of God's children. Remember Saph's power is limited to your desire to empower him. Remember that God has given you power to stump on the head of your giant, the power to overcome the enemy. Power that will lead to joy unspeakable but first you must lean not on your own understanding but trust God and make room for the intervention of God through the Holy Spirit.

Giants of destruction come in many different forms, however their forms are usually recognizable by the believer. For example, the dream buster generally presents itself as an immovable barrier, overwhelming odds or a series of unfortunate circumstances that seem to create such an inconvenience that we would rather just abandon our dream. I guess now is as good a time as any to share with you a piece of my journey. Admittedly, I have never been much of a handy man or one to engage in labor which required more physical labor than mental gymnastics. As a young man I can recall the many projects my father would take on around the house. Projects that either required the assistance of a skilled laborer or the unskilled fledgling efforts of an in house workforce, as part of the latter I was often required to assist in the building of a deck or a shed or a host of other projects. On top of that I used to suck my middle and index fingers. I sucked those babies until my freshman year of college. Nonetheless, I can recall my father telling me on more than one occasion that I would have to grow up to be real smart because I did not want to get my hands dirty. I agreed and began to read everything I could. I remember hearing about someone who read the dictionary so I did that. I remember going to the library and getting myself a library card and checking out the Mr. Science books. My thirst for knowledge was insatiable until I was exposed to the speeches of Dr. Martin Luther King, Jr. at which point I realized that there was a tremendous benefit to acquiring a formal education. This is when I realized I wanted to earn a Ph.D.

Needless to say there were a plethora of obstacles confronting a young African American man with such ambitions (immovable barriers). After all no one in my home had ever attended college, no one in my neighborhood had a Ph.D. They were all hard working blue collar, God fearing, household providers who relied on the generosity of General Motors to sustain a meaningful life. My parents believed in the merits of a good education and placed us in a local parochial school, they quickly acknowledged that I was different from my siblings as I thrived in this small yet caring environment. As I matriculated through the school there was an element that was yet missing. As I entered my senior year of high school I was confronted with what's next (overwhelming odds). My brothers had graduated and enlisted in the army and now it was my turn to make a decision. Much to my dismay my high school guidance counselor never talked to me about college nor shared information with me regarding college representatives visiting our small campus. Admittedly, by that time I found school to be pretty boring. I would study just enough to get a good grade on the test. I would study a day maybe two before the test because school came relatively easy to me. I now realize this too was part of God's plan for my life (series of unfortunate circumstances). On the night before I was expected to take the ACT I had a gig DJ'ing a house party. I got home at about 3:00 a.m. and had to report to a local high school to take the ACT at 8:00 a.m. I took the ACT and bombed, I literally resorted to flipping a coin utilizing the process of elimination to arrive at an answer. Talk about sabbatoging a dream. Needless to say college began to appear more and more distant. Well after looking at the options confronting me I decided to give the college thing one last try. You see I was very active in my community. I was part of the church and actively participated in a local youth group that focused on helping young men reach their potential. These guys would load up a bus of youngsters and take them to colleges and expose them to the possibility of becoming whatever they wanted to become. They were modern day Giant Slayers.

I reflected on what they had deposited in my life and decided I would go for it. I asked the mayor for a letter of character reference, secured one from my youth advisor and got on a bus and ventured to Central Michigan University seeking admittance. I presented myself to the admissions department and literally begged them to admit me. After they recalculated my grades from high school I thought for sure it was over. The admissions representative was extremely gracious and agreed to meet with me the next day. She asked if I would be available to meet with her the next day, I then stated that I would be there until I was admitted. She laughed and asked where I was staying, I told her I had no plans. She asked me how much money I had and made arrangements for me to stay in one of the dorm rooms. The next day I showed up. I could see God move, she said come in and have a seat. She asked me to tell her more about myself and why I wanted to attend Central Michigan University. For about an hour and half I shared my story. I told her about the immovable barriers, the overwhelming odds and the series of circumstances that led me to her office that day. I can vividly recall her taking the piece of paper she had previously prepared, into her hands and began to rip it to shreds.

Today, I am Desmon R. Daniel, Ph.D. As believers we must present ourselves as a living sacrifice allowing the Holy Spirit to intervene and speak to those who play a part in the fulfillment of our dreams. Ultimately, the desire to press beyond the destructive forces of immovable barriers, overwhelming odds and our own series of unfortunate circumstances rests in our hands. We have been given the power to slay Saph by allowing our God to intervene, by yielding to the scripture that tells us to acknowledge God in ALL our ways.

CHAPTER 5

Lahmi vs. Elhanan

II Samuel 21:19
(The Giant of Harassment vs.
The Grace of God)

II Samuel 21:19 (KJV) And there was again a battle in Gob; with the Philistines, where Elhanan the son of Jaare-oregim, a Bethlehemite, slew the brother of Goliath the Gittite, the staff of whose spear was like a weaver's beam.

(NIV) In another battle with the Philistines at Gob, Elhanan son of Jaare-Oregim the Bethlehemite killed Goliath the Gittite, who had a spear with a shaft like a weaver's rod.

(NLT) In still another battle against the Philistines at Gob. As they fought, Sibbecai from Hushah killed Saph, another descendant of the giants.

(NASB) There was a war with the Philistines at Gob, and Elhanan the son of Jaare-oregim the Bethlehemite killed Goliath the Gittite, the shaft of whose spear was like a weaver's beam.

Lahmi (lah'-mi or LAH migh) was a brother of Goliath and he too vowed to destroy David. Lahmi's name translates as warrior. Like many of his ancestors Lahmi made a solemn oath to utterly destroy David thereby laying siege on the entire kingdom or nation as it were. Lahmi represented harassment and his tool centered around his ability to get under the skin of his victim to drive them to the point of frustration and agitation to the extent that the victim would abandon their original intent and focus on the elimination of the source of their individual or collective irritation, thus taking them away from their original objective.

Lahmi has a warriors spirit and he is persistent in his endeavors. He could portray himself as a friend or reveal himself as a foe. In many cases it is difficult to discern his true nature until he is well within your personal space.

> **Don't be duped: Be still and know what is real and what is counterfeit.**

Today, I am mature enough both personally and spiritually to appreciate the Spirit of Elhanan (el HAY nun). Elhanan represents the "Grace of God" in fact his name means "God is Gracious." Who among us could live without the grace of an almighty God? Certainly not I, and if we are to be totally honest we have all benefited and are benefiting from God's grace even if it were expressed through a total non-believer as exemplified in the Book of Exodus wherein Pharoah showed grace unto Moses and the children of Israel. Although this grace was temporal, its expression lasted long enough for Moses and the children of Egypt to escape the boundary of the city. Sometimes all we need is a moment of grace, just enough grace to escape our situation, and in our escape we find the strength to make a different decision.

At one time in my journey I was blessed to serve as a substance abuse counselor. A client, we'll call her She-She for the sake of discussion, once shared a situation with me that I will never forget. She-She found herself in an abusive and harassing relationship with a man that she originally thought was the love of her life. Admittedly she had not been in many previous relationships and her relationship with her father was in her own words "cool." She often told me about how this young man came along and swept her off of her feet. Initially he was very attentive, however never truly complimentary. She-She once visited my office wearing a pair of sunglasses. Originally I presumed that she was trying to conceal bloodshot eyes, after all she was seeing me as a result of a court order for an alcohol related incident. Several minutes into the session, she removed the sunglasses only to reveal a swollen and bruised right eye. I made every effort to conceal my emotions as I calmly made note of my observation. I allowed her to continue to discuss treatment plans for several more minutes before interrupting her to ask "How are things at home?" She looked at me and confided in me that she allowed her boyfriend to move in with her since we last met and he became angry following a heated verbal exchange. I could almost see a smile arise on her face when she said she immediately asked him to leave. I imagine that her request was not as pleasant as she let on.

You see She-She had the appearance of a young woman well able to take care of herself. She was articulate and capable of verbalizing her deepest desires and dreams. In a previous session she shared her plans to go back to school to complete a degree in business management she had begun just over a year ago. Due to a series of unfortunate experiences she found herself out of school and working a couple of jobs that were more of a liability than an asset. She-She could not understand why she was going through such a challenge. Like many others, she stated that she informed the manager at the time of the interview that she would only be available in the evenings because she was a student and most of her classes required that she be in school during the day. Initially the work schedule accommodated her school schedule, however after a little while she found that her manager became more insistent that she make her job a priority. At first she figured she could sacrifice some of her study time to make some much needed money. The more she worked, the more she fell behind in her studies. After some time she accommodated the manager much to the detriment of her studies and she eventually withdrew from her courses.

It was during that time that She-she met the love of her life. She recalled going out to the bar more and more frequently after withdrawing from school. In fact this is where she met the love of her life. He was working part time as a bartender and he would often give her free drinks. She-She also admitted that she liked the extra attention. He would frequently call her place and ask if she had plans and if she was coming out to the bar after work. Having nothing else to do she would find herself relaxing at the bar. One night after leaving the bar on her way home, she noticed the flashing lights in her rearview mirror. Pulling over she recalled whispering a prayer within herself. The officer pulled her over for a broken tail light and during the course of the discussion he smelled alcohol on her breath which resulted in her required treatment.

This brings us to the bruised eye incident. I asked again, "So how are things at home?" She replied "well, he kept calling me and calling me so I let him come back. Things were o.k. for a while but last night he got angry and this is what happened." She slumped back in her seat, let out a huge sigh and said "I just need a moment of grace."

A moment of grace is sometimes all it takes for you to see clearly and plan your next step. In this case, as she took a moment to gather her thoughts, God's grace began to manifest itself through her own words. I could literally see God moving in her as she said, "I need to call the police so that I can get him out of my place. I will get a restraining order against him ....," I could see God's grace pouring out in her words. It all began with a moment of grace.

I can recall a much lighter example of Lahmi and Elhanan in my younger years. One day a group of friends and I, were taking a ride through a local park which we affectionately called the island. We were riding in an old beat up gas guzzler with welded doors, torn seats and rusted floor boards. Nonetheless, we were riding. Oh yeah, did I mention that there was no air conditioning. On this particular hot and sunny day at the park we spotted some young ladies whom we wanted to impress.

We rolled up the windows, and rolled some towels and a sheet over the holes in the floor board in an attempt to deter the cars fumes. We were cool but hot. We determined that all it would take is a couple of times around the park, a couple of inconspicuous passes and the young ladies would be innately forced to flag us down. Well somehow a fly invaded our space and began to harass us. We tried to play it cool, no pun intended, but the driver of our flagship could not escape the annoying and repetitive aerial assault of fly.

We could see the fly dart to and from his ear, forcing him to fling his arms violently as though convulsing. Eventually our captain abandoned the mission, threw the gear into park and jumped out of the car catching his loafer on the sheet ripping it from its strategically placed position giving rise to some overwhelming fumes which resulted in the collective abandonment of our mission.

In this situation Lahmi is represented by the common housefly. This small yet potentially powerful foe harassed us to the extent that we could not maintain our focus, our cool, our composure nor our physical space.

Isn't it interesting that sometimes in our journey we are disturbed by the littlest things? Small things occupy our mind and tie up our circuits to the extent that we become temporarily consumed by them which can result in the development of a strategy to utterly destroy our nuisance, thus taking us further off course than we originally intended. As we develop our strategy we are like Wild-E-Coyote employing all the Acme products we can afford instead praying for a moment of grace whereby we can refocus and pursue another course of action.

Elhanan was successful in the destruction of Lahmi and even today Elhanan can rise up within us to slay our harasser. Although Lahmi learned many of the same tricks as his brother Goliath who for 40 days harassed the children of God with his verbal assaults and physical prompts, Elhanan was still victorious. Lahmi's desire was to cause Elhanan to lose focus or use excessive force to address an issue which merely required the Grace of God.

God's grace allows us to somehow rise above our current situation and see life for what it is…a gift. A gift to be enjoyed, shared and cherished. Today we are living under God's dispensation of grace, such a dispensation merely requires our acceptance. Lahmi (harassment) wants us to take our eyes off of God's grace, abandon our mission and give up the car so that he can drive.

Submission to the harasser can result in a life of abuse or an acute case of depression because you have lost touch with your purpose, your mission, your quest. All it takes is a moment with Elhanan, a moment of grace to some how rise above and see it for what it is.

It's true that many of us believe that we are not worthy of the grace of God. Heck many of us never really knew or know what grace is. Let us end this query right now. Grace is the unmerited favor or kindness shown with no regard to who you are. Grace is one of the most precious and powerful attributes of God, which is often accompanied by or associated with mercy, love, compassion and patience when dealing with moments of extreme distress. In moments of intense distress grace is a source of help and deliverance. Thus, it is logical that God would send us grace to deal with the harassment of the enemy. Let us not for a moment think that the gift of grace is to be taken for granted. It is a gift granted to believers through the belief in our covenant relationship with Jesus Christ. This covenant is not like any simple contract with timelines or an end date. This covenant is a permanent arrangement which covers the believers entire being. Thus we should all seek to establish a covenant relationship with God so that we too can rise above our circumstance and slay the giants therein.

CHAPTER 6

The Unnamed Giant vs. Jonathan

II Samuel 21:20-21
(The Giant of a Flawed Humanity vs.
The Redemptive Power of God)

II Samuel 21:20-21 (KJV) 20 And there was a battle in Gath, where was a man of great stature, that had on every hand six fingers, and on every foot six toes, four and twenty in number; and he also was born to the giant. 21 And when he defied Israel, Jonathan the son of Shimea the brother of David slew him.

(NIV) 20 In still another battle, which took place at Gath, there was a huge man with six fingers on each

hand and six toes on each foot – twenty-four in all. He also was descended from Rapha.

(NLT) 20 In another battle with the Philistines at Gath, a huge man with six fingers on each hand and six toes on each foot – a descendant of the giants-21 defied and taunted Israel. But he was killed by Jonathan, the son of David's brother Shimea.

(NASB) 20 There was war at Gath again, where there was a man of great stature who had six fingers on each hand and six toes on each foot, twenty-four in number; and also had been born to the giant. 21 When he defied Israel, Jonathan the son of Shimei, David's brother, struck him down.

Decision/Dilemma

Have you ever wondered, just how many of God's children have "issues" which result from man's inhumanity to man? For those who believe that there is a divine order, it can be argued that the Israelites were being molded through their experiences. Perhaps these wars were a means of educating and developing character for future generations.

There is no human destructive force greater than that of war. Evidence of that historic fact has been chronicled in the Bible and continues to be experienced even today. Other destructive forces such as plagues, famine, fire and flood have also contributed to the destruction of generations of mankind. When we look at the damage man has done to mankind in the name of war it is enough to populate the world over again. Some might argue that mankind lives to war against itself due to some innate hatred for self or perhaps some deep seeded need to dominate. So once again we find that the Israelites are at war with the Philistines, this makes a total of 5 wars which is exactly the number of stones David once removed from the stream.

What is the significance of this unnamed giant? Who is he and why would he be considered as special? Let us briefly analyze his appearance. The Bible says he was a man of great stature not unlike all of the giants before him. So it would be logical to presume that this reference to his stature simply references the fact that he stands taller than the average man. The average height for a man is 5 foot 9 inches. Thus his stature is greater than average. That alone is worthy of acknowledgement, but not worthy of awe. Shaquille O'Neal "Shaq" stands 7 foot 1 inch and weighs about 325 pounds. He is a big guy. But it's not his height alone that makes him a standout basketball player. It's his ability to use his body to dominate his opponent in the game of basketball that makes him great. Taken out of this setting he may not be recognized as being of "great stature." For example the beverage commercial featuring Shaq riding a horse participating in a popular derby creates a level of cognitive dissonance that is simply comical. We know that the smaller the Jockey, the faster the horse can run by the mere virtue of the weight the horse is required to bear. Thus creating a more favorable opportunity for the horse to maximize its chances of running or reaching it's maximum speed. Thus, maximizing its capacity. In short a giant out of its natural element is a detriment to itself and can not be considered a threat and certainly not a being of great stature.

This fact exposes the first element of the un-named giants relevance. This giant exists to remind us of the importance of acknowledging the position of humankind in God's creation in the natural balance of things. Humankind has been given dominion over the things of this earth. Therefore, we are expected to be good stewards. Our failure to effectively govern the things of God will lead to an eventual imbalance in our midst, we seek to eliminate the threat. We wage war against that thing that we perceive as being the source of the discomfort. We seek to devour the dis-ease the source of our imbalance. We seek to take authority over the invader of our personal space and enforce our will over its existence. We seek to restore balance, we seek to restore what we perceive as being the natural harmony of the things which make our existence peaceful. Then we too can be characterized as being of "great stature."

The second element can be found through looking at the un-named giants hands and feet. He had 24 fingers and toes, 6 on each hand and foot. This guy was big and ill formed, which only means that his hands and feet were not normal. Six fingers on each hand, 6 toes on each foot. This is not normal. In today's economy he would be eligible for disability services. He might even be eligible for supplemental services in school. He would be eligible for money and support services to help him cope with the fact that he was not like everyone else. The purpose of the support services is to teach him to function just like everyone else in spite of his 24 toes and fingers.

The 24 fingers and toes appears to be more of a problem for the observer than it is for the person with the, so called disability. The truth is we are troubled by those things that do not fit our perception of the way things should be, creating a mental challenge some-times too difficult for us to overcome. Note the source of the difficulty is eternal. We have a difficult time perceiving things we do not understand as having a purpose. In reading the Bible I have yet to find that we were instructed to discover the purpose for all things. When I entered the work purpose in my computer a prompt appeared which read "searching for purpose." At that point my spirit quickened within me. The more I read and researched my findings made my days more enlightened and disturbing. More often than not when "purpose" appears in the Bible it is associated with evil. Because of our human condition we have developed evil purposes which disrupt the natural order of God's creation. We have purposed in our hearts that which we will do, become, accept and share based upon our personally developed purposes. Better yet we have done so without the benefit of wise counsel.

You see this un-named giant forces us to take an inventory of ourselves, our personal lives. At that time we are challenged to determine where exactly we fit in with God's creation. Where do I fit in, in God's natural order of things? Am I a living example of the manifestation of God's goodness, grace and mercy or am I the giant that stands in the way of God's plan? Is it I who needs to be slain for the sake of my family, my community, my country. **What value am I adding to God's kingdom on Earth?**

Jonathan, David's nephew, served as the secretary in David's royal cabinet. Jonathan was also considered one of David's chief warriors. His role of secretary exposed him to a vast body of knowledge, he was allowed to attend meetings called by the King himself wherein the counsel would assemble to discuss the issues of the day. Jonathan, by virtue of his role within the cabinet was able to hear, analyze, and chronicle the collective thoughts of the entire body. After carefully reviewing all that had been said he realized it was in the best interest of the body to slay the un-named giant in order that the purpose of the body might be born into existence.

Jonathan realized and accepted his call to war against a giant that represented a flawed human condition. Arguably, this giant existed to call us to look at ourselves and unequivocally determine that we are not perfect, we are not self-sustaining however we do have the capacity to thrive if and when we find ourselves in our created place in the world.

The simple truth is that we will continue to be confronted by the giants, the challenge is determining how to react to their presence and better still how to prepare for the arrival of the next one. The Bible clearly instructs us to acknowledge God in all of our ways, we are encouraged to treat others as we desire to be treated. These words are more than just quant sayings or clichés that we can conveniently call out when we feel comfortable, they must be purposely rooted in our hearts. We must develop a made up mind wherein we will intentionally act in a manner which supports our belief system.

The process of bringing any ideal, dream or concept into fruition requires a rigorous journey of the mind. You become a force of disillusion, you can and often do, think of the reasons or excuses to stop progress. You may think of your personal limitations, prohibitions and various other self perpetuated doubts. However, in spite of all this you must press on toward the mark.

At the point that you choose to expose your ideal to others, some will begin to rally around the notion that your ideal is fool-hearted. Some may say that it was ill conceived and utterly ridiculous. Now is when you must raise up and confront them because they stand in opposition of your goal. At that point you have the opportunity to expand your group of followers to include the likes of Abishai, Sibbecai, Elhanan, and Jonathan all of whom stand ready to give their very existence to support your cause.

CHAPTER 7

Mobile Army Surgical Hospital

In times of war it is understood that many soldiers will lose their lives as they engage in battle for their respective cause. Although the loss of life is generally expected as humans engage in physical combat which is not at all limited to swords, spears and other such weaponry that is currently thought to be archaic; every warring faction has its own medical staff whose goal is to sustain the life of the soldier. A more sufficient example of this service can be found by reviewing the following; in 1968 author Richard Hooker published MASH: A Novel About Three Army Doctors, in 1970 a dark comedic film MASH appeared on the scene followed by a televisions series which also ran for a number of years (all of which were fictional treatments on the subject). The United States Army medical unit has been called MASH, short for Mobile Army Surgical Hospital. This army unit serves as a hospital in the midst of a combat area.

Hooker, a former military surgeon, knew that the general mission of a hospital is to provide some level of care to those who have been physically, emotionally and or spiritually wounded in the course of their life. Additionally, a hospital strives to provide health services and facilities that will promote wellness, relieve human suffering and to restore an individual to good health in a timely and efficient manner while expressing a value for all those in need of care. That being the case a M.A.S.H. unit must therefore be trained to respond to a crisis in the midst of turmoil. It is understood that the mortality rate is heavily influenced by the ability to remove the soldier from the field of war, take them to a designated area wherein coordinated care can be rendered to the injured party. It is presumed that reasonable resources will be on hand and utilized in the treatment of the persons injuries. Today, arguably this is the quintessential function of the Trauma Center. Simply put there is a Trauma Center on every battlefield, with a specific goal to save lives.

So as we seek to employ the services of the virtues ascribed to Abishai, Sibbecai, Elhanan, and Jonathan it is equally as important to know that there is someone waiting to nurse them back to good health so that they too can return to the battlefield on our behalf. As disciples and Giant Slayers we are called to serve in the capacity of the M.A.S.H. unit, our churches are called to serve in the capacity of the M.A.S.H. and our churches are in need of skilled surgeons, trauma units, medics, first responders and the like. There will be times that we will be required to service others and at times we will require the services of other disciples as we continue our respective journey. With this in mind it is imperative that we take heed to what our ancestors have gone through or at a minimum we should learn from our own mistakes, misgivings and misperceptions of the world around us. Our respective training comes through a succession of life experiences ultimately designed to equip us for the journey ahead. It is only by grace that we are not consumed by the many issues confronting us.

It has been said that grace is getting what you did/

do not deserve, and mercy is not getting what you do deserve. That being said, the M.A.S.H. unit is comprised of real people just like you and me. There challenge is to get through their stuff while also helping us get through ours. M.A.S.H. unit personnel are professionals who in spite of themselves have been granted grace and mercy sufficient to meet the needs of the moment. If the moment requires a blood transfusion, they are prepared to handle it. If the moment requires stitches, they are prepared to handle it. If the moment requires, amputation, they are prepared to handle it. Whatever the moment requires they are prepared to handle, yet amazingly the victim rarely if ever recognizes them once the service has been rendered and they awaken in the recovery area.

Just like the soldier the M.A.S.H. unit personnel do not seek recognition for what they do, they are driven by a cause greater than themselves. Please believe that Abishai, Sibbecai, Elhanon and Jonathan never sought to be recognized for their bravery. They merely wanted to do what was right in the eyes of their king and their countrymen. As we engage the Giants in our lives, keep your eyes on the big picture. Know that the King of Kings is watching you and your countrymen are relying on you. By maintaining your focus on the big picture you too will be able to withstand the fiery darts of the enemy. You too will be granted the gifts of Grace & Mercy to add to your satchel.

"A Luta Continua a Victoria e Certa"
The Struggle continues but victory is certain

There are giants which yet exist. Many of the giants of today share common characteristics with those we find in scripture. Some of the giants of today are best known by the characteristics of harassment, destruction, prejudice, racism, inhumanity, sexism, intolerance, elitism and a host of other ism's. All believers have the capacity to become "Giant Slayers" in their own right. The community activist who champions the cause to eradicate drug trafficking has the capacity to be a giant slayer. The teacher who works tenaciously to teach students to read and write has the capacity. The single parent whom enrolls in college to better their employability skills, has the capacity. The fireman who courageously enters a burning house to retrieve a fear struck family or the armed service person who wars on foreign soil to protect the freedom of their country and introduce a better way of life to others. All of these fierce warriors are giant slayers fighting for change.

Change comes through various movements, some of which are the result of physical war; yet none are more or less important than the other. As our nation embraced the need for change through the democratic process of voting wherein Barack Obama was elected President of the United States, we recognized the need for another Giant Slayer. Just as in the case of David and Goliath... the struggle continues; beyond our current generation and into the future, however one thing is certain... victory belongs to the believer.

Work Cited

Bell, J. S. & Campbell S. (2005). The Complete Idiots Guide to The Bible, 3rd edition. Alpha Books.

The Holy Bible, New International Version. Zondervan. Grand Rapids, Michigan. 2005. Print.

The Holy Bible, New Living Translation. Tyndale House Publishers, Inc. Carol Stream, Illionis. 2004. Print.

Zondervan Full Life Study Bible - New International Version. The Zondervan Corporation, Grand Rapids, Michigan. 1992. Print.

Zondervan NASB Study Bible, Kenneth L. Barker, gen. ed. Grand Rapids, MI: Zondervan, 1999. Print.

Zondervan Amplified, KJV, NASB & NIV Comparative Study Bible. Grand Rapids, MI: Zondervan, 1999. Print.

LaVergne, TN USA
28 January 2010
171445LV00001B/2/P